OVERVIEW

Overview

Making professional propositions is an ability that's common to most successful entrepreneurs and bubooksinesspeople – and this is what cold calling is all about. A cold call is the first call you make to a prospective customer. The customer isn't expecting your call, so no preliminary work has yet been done. It's through cold calling that businesspeople open new doors and generate leads for sales.

Although making cold calls may be daunting initially, it's only by doing it that you'll generate new sales leads for your business.

Learning the art of making effective cold calls will also add to your career prospects, enhancing your sales successes no matter which market and business arena you move into.

This book focuses on several skills you should have when making effective cold calls that lead to appointments and new business:

- assess your cold call script and find ways to improve it,
- identify key times to call prospects,
- deal with gatekeepers effectively, and
- overcome common objections that prospects may raise during a cold call.

As you practice and hone your cold-calling skills, your confidence will grow. You'll handle potential rejections better and you'll experience fewer of them. And as a result, you'll be better positioned to generate sales.

You may be a master of the sales pitch and your persuasive abilities may be without fault. But if the person you're talking to doesn't need what you're offering, you're just wasting time. That's why it's important to evaluate prospects before you contact them. What you want to avoid is calling everyone on a long contact list in the hope that you'll reach someone who's interested.

You need to qualify sales prospects or leads. This means determining who's likely to purchase the product or service you're selling.

It's these people you want to focus your sales efforts on.

You need to find out their requirements so you have appropriate solutions to offer. When you take this kind of approach, it increases your chances of making a sale.

In this book, you'll learn what initial planning and research you should perform to qualify a prospect. You'll learn why it's important to conduct a qualification meeting and how to do this effectively. Finally, you'll learn how best to develop a lead you've qualified into a sales opportunity.

In sales, there's no point in doing your preparation, contacting a prospect, and delivering a first-class presentation unless you get the result you're after – to close the sale. But to seal the deal, you should use specific strategies that can help you succeed in the final stages.

For example, you'll need to leverage your value proposition in a way that convinces prospects to take action.

You'll need to time your closing properly. To do this, you'll need to recognize certain signals that the prospect is ready to buy.

And you'll have to use an appropriate closing technique, given the situation. In this book, you'll learn essential principles for closing a sale:

- how to develop a strong and effective value proposition,
- how to recognize when a prospect is ready to close based on the signs the prospect gives you,
- how to deal with sales objections appropriately,
- which key strategies you can use to close a sale, and
- how to follow up with the customer after the sale is complete.

By learning and applying these principles, you'll improve your selling skills and enhance your reputation in the minds of your customers.

CHAPTER I - MASTERING COLD CALLING

CHAPTER I - Mastering Cold Calling

This chapter focuses on several skills you should have when making effective cold calls that lead to appointments and new business:
- assess your cold call script and find ways to improve it,
- identify key times to call prospects,
- deal with gatekeepers effectively, and
- overcome common objections that prospects may raise during a cold call.

As you practice and hone your cold-calling skills, your confidence will grow. You'll handle potential rejections better and you'll experience fewer of them. And as a result, you'll be better positioned to generate sales.

AN EFFECTIVE COLD-CALLING SCRIPT

An effective cold-calling script

Why develop a script?
Cold calling can be daunting. That's because it involves calling someone you don't know – and this person may reject an offer you make or even become annoyed and refuse to continue speaking to you. However, with the right planning, you can boost your confidence and your success rate, helping ensure that cold calls lead to new business relationships for you and your company.

Janice is an insurance broker for Callinsure Insurance Corporation. She's using cold calling in an attempt to secure meetings with potential corporate clients.

Follow along as Janice calls Alex at Docu-Sentry.

Janice: Hi. Is that Alex? Alex Chung? *Janice asks a little hesitantly.*

Alex: Yes? Alex here. *Alex responds in a neutral tone.*

Janice: I'm Janice from Callinsure – a large insurance firm with a great range of packages you might be interested in... *Janice speaks quickly and enthusiastically.*

Alex: Are you trying to sell insurance to me or my company? *Alex, annoyed, interjects.*

Janice: That's the great thing – we have individual and corporate packages. As an IT manufacturer you might be interested in coverage for industrial accidents... *Janice continues.*

Alex: Industrial accidents? I don't think so. We're an IT solutions provider. And you know what? We already have good coverage. So, no thanks. *Alex interjects angrily.*

Janice: Oh. I see. Well thanks for your time. *Janice responds dejectedly.*

Janice didn't do her homework for this call. She didn't research Docu-Sentry's needs or even find out what the company does. During the call, she also seemed to focus more on her company's products than on the goal of the call – which was to set up a meeting.

A successful cold call depends on proper preparation. Before making the call, you should set a goal for it.

It's helpful to conduct some preliminary research about the prospective customer you're planning to call. For example, search online for information about the successes and challenges that the prospect is facing. Useful sources of this information might include a company's annual report or press releases, or product descriptions on its web site.

It may also be possible to speak to your prospect's customers to determine areas where the prospect's service could improve, or to speak to the prospect's employees to find out what challenges they face.

Too many salespeople focus only on the products they're offering or on their own companies during cold calls. Instead you should focus on a prospect's business pressures and challenges, and on how what you have to offer could help address these. This is the best way to create interest. But it takes some thought and planning. Scripting your calls can help.

Advantages of scripting calls

You may have noted that if you have a basic script to work from, you'll have more control during the call and more confidence.

You can draw on your own and others' experiences to develop a script that's effective, and that suits your personality and style. Using the script will ensure consistency in your approach. It will also increase the likelihood that you'll succeed in securing appointments with your prospects.

Scripts will vary for different prospects, and you'll still have to provide impromptu answers and make quick decisions during calls. You don't want to just read out a script in an unnatural way.

Create a sketch of what you want to say – with important details and points – but be prepared to deviate from them when necessary.

Assessing script openings

When developing your script for a cold call, remember that the way you open the call is a determining factor in whether the person will want to continue with the call. So it's critical to include an effective opening in your script. This involves three steps. First capture the prospect's attention. Then identify yourself and your company. And third, state the reason for your call.

Avoid using gimmicks to capture the prospect's attention. Instead, use the prospect's name, and keep the opening of your call short and conversational.

See each guideline for opening a cold call for more information about it.

Avoid gimmicks

Suppose someone you don't know starts a call by telling you that you've been selected as the lucky winner of a prize. Would you trust the person? Or would you be on your guard?

Misleading someone, lying, or using gimmicks sets the wrong tone for a conversation and makes it more likely that your proposition will be rejected. So avoid using these tactics in an attempt to gain a prospect's attention.

Using the prospect's name

The best way to begin a cold call is with a simple greeting in which you use the prospect's name. Opening with "Hello Maria" or "Hello Ms. Chavez," for example, gets your prospect's attention and sets the stage for a polite and intelligent conversation. It also makes it more likely you'll receive a positive response.

Keep the opening short and conversational

There's no universal technique for capturing a prospect's interest. However, you need to do this quickly and simply at the start of a cold call. The best approach is to keep your opening polite, short, and conversational.

If you take too much time before identifying yourself and getting to the point, it may seem like you don't want to reveal your real purpose – and your call is likely to be rejected.

Question

Essential Selling Skills

Which examples of dialog do you think are likely to succeed in capturing a prospect's attention?

Options:

1. "Hello Jerry. I read that your company has recently expanded and is setting up a new branch in our city. Congratulations!"

2. "Hello. Could I speak to Susan please? Hi Susan, this is Hitoshi from Med Imps."

3. "Hi. This is Martin from Callinsure. I have some great insurance options for you."

4. "Hi is that Imogene? ...Oh I must have dialed the wrong number, but since I have you on the line, can I interest you in a great financial package?"

Answer:

Option 1: This is a correct option. This caller is likely to capture the prospect's attention because she uses the person's name and shows knowledge of his company.

Option 2: This option is correct. Here the speaker uses the prospect's name to gain her attention, and is polite and conversational.

Option 3: This option is incorrect. Martin fails to use the prospect's name to gain attention and goes straight into selling, rather than starting a polite conversation with the prospect.

Option 4: This is an incorrect option. Here the caller uses a "wrong number" gimmick to begin the conversation and then moves straight into trying to make a sale. This approach is unlikely to be successful.

Once you have a prospect's attention, you need to identify yourself. State your name and the name of your company. You could also provide a brief "commercial," or promotional overview of your company. For example, you might say "We're a global financial solutions company working with over 20 listed companies worldwide." However, don't be tempted to talk too much at this point. Make it your goal to learn about the prospect and how you might be able to help.

Next, it's a good idea to use a question to start the conversation in a nonthreatening way and put everyone at ease. The question shouldn't take much thought to answer or require a lengthy response. It might be something as simple as "How are you today?"

Cold calls should be short and to the point. So after a brief icebreaker, state the reason for your call. Typically your goal will be to set an appointment with the prospect – and you should make this clear from the outset. However, you also need to clarify why the prospect should consider meeting with you. You do this by linking what you have to offer to your prospect's business needs.

For instance, you might say something like "I'd like to set up an appointment with you to discuss ways we can help you streamline your supply chain." You've identified the potential benefit of a meeting for the prospect.

A statement like "I'd like to meet with you to tell you about the ground-breaking supply management software we sell" is less effective. This is because it focuses on you and your company. It makes it clear what you want – which is to sell software – instead of focusing on how the prospect could benefit.

If relevant, it can be effective to state that you've been working with companies in the prospect's industry, especially if you can name one or more high-profile companies the prospect is likely to be familiar with.

Alternatively, you might refer to projects you've been working on that address needs similar to those of the prospect's company.

In both cases, this helps make it clear that you have something relevant to offer and that it's worth the prospect's time to meet with you.

Question

Match the conversation fragments to the corresponding step of the process for making an effective cold call.

Options:

A. "Hello Jane."

B. "It's Yusuf here from Callinsure – we offer a range of insurance packages for the medical industry worldwide. How are you?"

C. "I'm calling to set up an appointment, to discuss how you can optimize your insurance options in light of the new privacy legislation."

Targets:

1. Step 1
2. Step 2
3. Step 3

Answer:

Greeting a prospect by name is a simple and effective strategy for gaining the prospect's attention, which is the first step in a scripted cold call.

In the second step of a scripted cold call, you introduce yourself and your company. You may also include a brief promotion of your company and ask "How are you?" to get the conversation started.

In the third step, you state the purpose of your call – to set up a meeting. At this stage, you should make it clear how meeting with you could benefit the prospect.

Assessing script closings

Once you've successfully negotiated the first three steps of a cold call, you can move on to the final two phases – asking questions and setting the appointment.

During a cold call, you should use open-ended questions, which require more than just single-word responses. Such questions help you uncover the prospect's business needs so you can link these to what you can provide. For example, you might say that other clients are struggling to reduce malware downloads on their cell phones. You could then ask what kind of IT security issues the prospect is facing.

Closed-ended questions may not be as effective as open-ended ones. You need the prospect to talk to you rather than simply providing "yes" or "no" answers.

Also avoid asking rhetorical or leading questions, like "Would you like to increase your sales by up to 10%?" This comes across as a gimmick, and won't help you uncover a specific business need you can help address.

Question

You're scripting a cold call for selling financial services to customers.

Which examples of questions are appropriate?

Options:

1. "We have a broad range of financial products that you could invest in. Are you interested in investing in stocks and bonds?"

2. "Several of our clients have found it difficult to vet potential stock investments against ethical business standards. What challenges are you facing?"

3. "Our customers' average returns on investments over the year are at around 16%, despite the recession. What range of returns have you been earning on your investments recently?"

4. "Are you happy with your current stockbroker?"

Answer:

Option 1: This option is incorrect. This is a closed-ended question that can be answered with a "yes" or "no." It doesn't encourage the prospect to talk to you or to reveal specific business needs.

Option 2: This is a correct option. This approach attempts to link a challenge the prospect may be facing with what the cold caller can do to resolve the challenge. It also opens the door for the prospect to discuss what the business challenges really are.

Option 3: This option is correct. Mentioning the recession may link to the prospect's current challenges. Also, the question is an open-ended one, inviting the prospect to talk to the cold caller rather than just providing "yes" or "no" responses.

Option 4: This is an incorrect option. This is a closed-ended question that invites a "yes" or "no" answer.

To prepare for setting an appointment, you should determine two dates and times when it will be convenient for you to meet with the prospect. During the call, you can then take the lead, suggesting a meeting time and providing an alternative if necessary. You should also indicate roughly how long the meeting will take.

For example, you might say something like "I'm in the area on Thursday. We could meet at 10 a.m. – it should take half an hour to review your current system and to identify where we can improve it. Would that suit you?"

This approach places the focus on when the prospect will meet you – rather than if the prospect will meet you. So it makes it less likely that the prospect will refuse to proceed with a meeting.

If the prospect turns down your first and second suggestions for meeting dates and times, you can ask the prospect to suggest a meeting time as a last resort.

Implementing the five steps

Maggie is a sales consultant for a pharmaceutical company. She's looking for opportunities to secure new clients for her company.

Follow along as Maggie completes a cold call, noting how she implements all five steps of the call.

Maggie: Hello. Could I speak to David? *Maggie asks calmly and confidently.*

David: Speaking. *David responds neutrally.*

Maggie: Hi David. It's Maggie here from Gleeson's Associates. How are you today? *Maggie is friendly and smiling.*

David: I'm fine... What company did you say you were from? *David responds with a little confusion.*

Maggie: Gleeson's, a global pharmaceutical supplier for two of your local hospitals. *Maggie continues confidently.*

David: I see.

Maggie: We run projects to help companies comply with the new reporting laws. I'd like to meet with you to talk about how you're doing – those new requirements can be confusing – don't you think?

David: I know what you mean but we don't have any issues. All set on our end. *David interrupts Maggie.*

Maggie: That's great! But what about delivery times? Have those been affected by the new documentation requirements? *Maggie continues enthusiastically.*

David: Well... yes. It has been a problem. *David concedes.*

Maggie: I'll be in the area on Monday the 11th. I could fit in a meeting with you at...say 10:30? If we give ourselves half an hour to 45 minutes, we can discuss some possible solutions. *Maggie sounds calm and professional.*

David: I have a meeting on Monday morning. *David is slightly hesitant.*

Maggie: OK. Let's see – how is Tuesday the 12th at 2:00 p.m.? *Maggie remains upbeat.*

David: Let me just check my calendar...OK – I have half an hour free then. David looks at his schedule and agrees. *David looks at his schedule and agrees.*

Maggie: Wonderful. I'm looking forward to meeting you. *Maggie closes warmly.*

Maggie successfully used all five steps in her script to set up a meeting. However, there's always room for improvement. For the best results, it's important to continually improve and edit your script. You can use each call to help further refine your technique.

Case Study: Question 1 of 2
Scenario

Hannah is a consultant for an information technology and telecommunications security company. She has created a script for use in cold calling financial institutions. She hopes to secure face-to-face appointments with prospects at these institutions.

Access the learning aid Phlogistix to help you answer the questions. Answer the questions in the given order.

Question

Why is Hannah's script ineffective?

Options:

1. She uses a gimmicky opening
2. She doesn't use questions effectively
3. She doesn't state her purpose up front but leaves that for later in the script
4. She should ask when the prospect is free before suggesting a meeting time

Answer:

Option 1: This option is correct. Opening with a rhetorical question like "How would you like two extra hours every day to get things done?" is gimmicky and unlikely to capture the prospect's interest.

Option 2: This option is incorrect. Hannah's questions are open-ended and focused on the prospect's business needs. They address common network security issues and are a good start to a conversation that could link her products to the prospect's business concerns.

Option 3: This option is correct. After introducing herself, Hannah should state the purpose of her call – to set up a face-to-face appointment – instead of trying to sell her company's product immediately, over the phone.

Option 4: This option is incorrect. It's better to offer a specific time and date for a meeting than to leave this to the prospect.

Case Study: Question 2 of 2

Which question could Hannah use to improve her script?

Options:

1. "How would you like us to do a complete overview of your security system?"

2. At the start, say "Hi Gerald, how are you today?"

3. "Would you like to spend less time every week worrying about network security?"

4. "What date and time are you free to meet with me?"

Answer:

Option 1: This option is incorrect. Hannah's current questions are effective. They let her explore the prospect's business needs and how these could be addressed. She shouldn't try selling during a cold call. She should simply set up a meeting.

Option 2: This is the correct option. Hannah should gain the prospect's attention without using gimmicks or generalized claims about her company.

Option 3: This option is incorrect. This question is gimmicky, and doesn't assess the client's real security needs.

Using a script for the cold calls you make can give you more control and more confidence. It enables a consistent approach and helps ensure that your calls are a success.

In the script for a cold call, you should begin by capturing the prospect's attention, introducing yourself and your company, and specifying that the purpose of your call is to set up a meeting.

You should then ask open-ended questions to find out more about the prospect's business needs and how your company can help in addressing these. Finally, suggest a time and date for an appointment.

WHEN NOT TO CALL A PROSPECT

When not to call a prospect

Timing a cold call

Timing is an important factor in the success of a cold call. It can be easy to overlook this. But if you call at the wrong time, it's more likely that a prospect will be impatient, annoyed by the disruption, and unwilling to hear you out. You can't know exactly when a prospect will be busy, but you can follow some general guidelines.

Most businesses are busier at certain times than at others. For example, retailers are likely to be busy mid-morning and in the late afternoon, whereas car service businesses are busiest early in the morning. It pays to know the business patterns of a prospect's company so you can avoid calling at the busiest times.

Similarly, you should try to analyze the company's business cycle and establish busy and slack periods. For example, retailers and hotels are likely to be busier during holiday seasons. They generally have time to regroup –

and to consider new services and products – after these times.

Question

Your company sells accounting software, and you're planning on using a cold call to approach a medium-sized accounting firm.

It's currently two weeks before the end of the tax year. Would this be a good time to call?

Options:

1. Yes
2. No

Answer:

The period leading up to the end of the tax year is likely to be the busiest time of the year for the accounting firm, so it's not a good time to place a cold call.

Timing rules are flexible and experienced sales people may disagree about when it's best to call. However, you should generally avoid making cold calls during certain times or days:

- before 8:00 a.m. – people may be unavailable or busy setting up what they need to do for the day,
- on Monday mornings, when people are typically busier than usual and catching up after the weekend,
- the day after a three-day holiday, when people are busy catching up, and
- the week before and after Christmas – because people are preparing for shutdowns or catching up after a break.

Between 10:00 and 11:40 a.m., people have usually settled in at work and are more receptive. However, it's also when people typically receive the most phone calls.

To make more of an impact, it may be preferable to call later in the day. Calls during nonbusiness hours aren't always welcomed but can sometimes be particularly successful – especially if it's a business owner or top executive you need to contact. These people are likely to have fewer distractions outside business hours.

Question

When is it generally advisable not to make a cold call?

Options:

1. Before 8:00 a.m.
2. On Monday mornings
3. The day after a three-day holiday
4. The weeks immediately before and after Christmas
5. In the early afternoon
6. Half an hour before lunch

Answer:

Option 1: This option is correct. Businesspeople are often unavailable or busy preparing for the coming workday before 8:00 a.m. So you shouldn't generally place cold calls before this time.

Option 2: This is a correct option. On Monday mornings, businesspeople typically need to catch up and organize their work for the coming week. This isn't a suitable time to make cold calls.

Option 3: This option is correct. People are usually busy catching up on the day after a three-day holiday and don't have time for additional considerations. So this isn't a good time for making cold calls.

Option 4: This is a correct option. In the week before Christmas, people are often rushing to finish work before their companies close. In the week after a Christmas break, they're usually busy catching up and preparing for the coming year. So these aren't good times for making cold calls.

Option 5: This option is incorrect. Early afternoon is generally a good time to make cold calls. This isn't an especially rushed time for most businesspeople.

Option 6: This is an incorrect option. Half an hour before lunch is an appropriate time to call. People are generally very receptive to calls between around 10:00 a.m. and 11:40 a.m. However, this is also when they receive the most calls – which can reduce the impact you have.

DEALING WITH GATEKEEPERS

Dealing with gatekeepers

Even when you time your call well, you may find it difficult to get through to the person you want to because of a persistent gatekeeper. A gatekeeper is someone who fields calls for the prospect you want to contact. For instance, this may be a personal assistant, receptionist, or administrator. Salespeople may be frustrated by gatekeepers who sometimes block access to the decision makers they want to reach.

Gatekeepers decide whether to allow you access to decision makers. So when speaking to a gatekeeper, you should treat that person with the same respect as you would the prospect you're hoping to reach.

Being evasive, lying, or otherwise disrespecting a gatekeeper lowers your chance of a successful interaction with your prospect, and may prevent you from accessing the prospect at all.

To get gatekeepers on your side, you need to work with them. For the best results, you should be confident and conversational, use your and the gatekeeper's names, and state your purpose in calling – which is generally to speak to the prospect to set up a meeting.

See each guideline for getting past gatekeepers for more information about it.

Be confident and conversational

If you're hesitant, anxious, apologetic, or unsure, your tone is likely to reflect this. It may be overly formal, for example, when you most want to be conversational. Being clear, confident, and polite will help you get the support you need from the gatekeepers.

So avoid apologies for disturbing a gatekeeper, and be confident that you're offering something of value. For example "Hello, I hope I'm not disturbing you, but would it be possible..." indicates hesitancy and a lack of confidence.

Use your and the gatekeeper's names

Gatekeepers most often answer the phone by giving a company name followed by their own name. When you get through to a gatekeeper, listen out for the person's name and use it to gain the gatekeeper's attention. You should also say your own name up front and try to research what your prospects' names are and ask for them by their first name.

For example, saying "Hi Julio, it's Sam Morton. Can you put me through to Alice in Accounting?" is far more likely to be effective than just saying "Hi, can you put me through to the head of Accounting please?"

State your purpose

Sales people may lie about their purpose to get past gatekeepers – for example by saying they're returning a call or using some other ruse. However, lying breaches trust and may damage your chances of reaching a prospect or forming a business relationship once you do.

Instead, you should briefly state your real purpose, of setting an appointment with your prospect. Avoid trying to sell a product or service to the gatekeeper. For example, state that you want to set an appointment "in relation to stock investment portfolios," rather than saying that your company offers the best custom stock portfolios and that you want to design a portfolio for the prospect.

Dealing effectively with gatekeepers

Janice from Callinsure wants to place a cold call to Linda, a department manager at a company called Sharp-End Tools. Martin, the gatekeeper, answers her call.

Follow along as Janice speaks to Martin.

Martin: Sharp-End Tools, Martin speaking. *Martin answers the call, in a neutral tone.*

Janice: Hi Martin. My name's Janice, and I work for Callinsure. Could you put me through to Linda in Human Resources please? *Janice speaks with a confident and friendly tone.*

Martin: What's it in connection with? *Martin hesitates.*

Janice: It's to set up an appointment with her to discuss insurance options for employees.

Martin: Would you like me to set up an appointment? *Martin is more relaxed.*

Janice: No thanks, Martin. I'd like to speak to Linda directly. *Janice is firm but polite.*

Martin: OK. I'm connecting you now. *Martin's tone is neutral.*

Janice did an excellent job in her conversation with the gatekeeper. Her tone was confident, she identified herself by name and used Martin's name, and made her purpose clear – without attempting to promote any product or service to the gatekeeper.

If a gatekeeper turns you away, you can use e-mail in an attempt to contact a prospect directly. In this case, you need to personalize the e-mail message for the prospect, saying that you're determined to speak with the prospect, and give a brief explanation of why. Ensure that your explanation shows clearly how your product or service has the potential to meet the prospect's business needs.

Question

Which call openings are good examples of how to get past a gatekeeper when you're making a cold call?

Options:

1. "Oh, hi. I was trying to get through to the head of the Finance Department. I was wondering if you could help me? My name's Justin."

2. "Hello there. This is Bhadrak from the Managec Group. We offer complete computer systems installation, support, and training. I'm hoping to speak to someone in IT, if that's possible."

3. "Hi Angela. This is Lila from Diallonics. May I please speak to Terence in Marketing? It's in relation to integrating phone and Internet communications."

4. "Hello Mario. It's Alice from Brocadero. Could you please put me through to Rhonda in Manufacturing? It's about calibrating equipment."

Answer:

Option 1: This option is incorrect. The caller in this case conveys a lack of confidence. He also hasn't used his or the gatekeeper's names, or stated his purpose in trying to reach the head of the Finance Department.

Option 2: This is an incorrect option. Although Bhadrak gives his name up front, he doesn't use the gatekeeper's or the prospect's names. He shouldn't be trying to promote his company's services to the gatekeeper. In addition, he seems hesitant in stating his purpose in speaking to the IT person.

Option 3: This option is correct. Lila conveys confidence. She states who she is, uses the gatekeeper's and the prospect's names, and states her purpose clearly.

Option 4: This is a correct option. Alice speaks with confidence, makes use of all relevant names, and states her purpose clearly and succinctly.

To improve your chances of success with cold calling, you need to time your calls appropriately. This involves avoiding times when prospects are most likely to be busy or preoccupied.

You also need to handle gatekeepers appropriately, or they may prevent you from speaking directly to prospects. To do this, you need to be polite and respectful. You should also state your name and use the gatekeeper's name, and state the purpose of your call without attempting to promote or sell anything directly to the gatekeeper.

OVERCOMING COLD-CALLING OBJECTIONS

Overcoming cold-calling objections

Common objections

Maggie is a sales consultant for a pharmaceutical company, and is using cold calls in an attempt to secure new clients. She is speaking with a client for whom her company could supply compliance training for new health and medical reporting legislation.

Follow along as Maggie tries to set up a meeting with the client representative, Lucas.

Maggie: I'd like to set up a meeting to discuss training options for compliance with the new health... *Maggie speaks with confidence but is interrupted by Lucas.*

Lucas: Afraid you've missed the boat on that one. We're creating our own training. *Lucas responds, smiling but dismissive.*

Maggie: Oh. I see. Well ...ah...thanks for your time. *Maggie is unsure of what to say.*

When preparing to make cold calls, it's important to plan how you'll respond to a range of possible objections prospects may have to meeting with you.

Lucas's response leaves Maggie uncertain about what to say next, so she ends the conversation and loses out on a potential opportunity.

She may have been confused when Lucas's response didn't align with her script. But scripts should guide your call not dictate it. You also need to be flexible – and to have strategies in place for handling a prospect's possible responses.

Although you can't counter all objections a prospect may have, you can ask questions. Find out what's really behind an objection and whether there's a possibility you can overcome it – for instance, because your company can provide more value than a competitor.

Common objections that you may face when cold calling include "We're happy with what we have," "I'm not interested," "I'm too busy," "We already have a supplier," and "The price is too high." These objections may be voiced differently, but with the same underlying messages.

See each of the common objection types for examples of how they may be phrased.

"Happy with what we have"

Prospects whose companies are already using a product or service that's similar to the one you offer might say "We already have a project underway," "We're happy with the coverage we have," "We already have managed investments," "Training is already on the go," or something similar.

This type of response indicates that a prospect needs and wants products or services like yours, so this is a potential opportunity.

"Not interested"

Prospects might say they're not interested, have no need for your products or services, or won't benefit from them.

In these cases, you have an opportunity to find out why they believe this and to explain how your product or service really could be of benefit.

"Too busy"

The "too busy" objection is quite common. It's often accompanied by a request that you send information rather than continuing a conversation or meeting the prospect in person. Information sent in this way is often discarded without even being read.

As an example, a prospect may say "I'm on my way to a meeting," "We've got too much work at the moment, so if you just send me the information I'll go through it when I have a chance," or even "I can't waste my time with this."

Other phrases that can alert you to this type of objection are ones that try to postpone further discussion – for example, "I'll get back to you once we have the new budgets."

"Already have a supplier"

Prospects may say that they have an existing relationship or a great program, are working with the competition, or are happy with their current suppliers' work. This objection provides an opportunity to identify a niche or unfulfilled need.

"Price is too high"

When prospects say things like "We haven't got a budget for that," "Our current supplier gives a more reasonable rate," or "The expense isn't justified," they fall into the "price is too high" category.

With this objection, your role is to focus on showing the value of the offering to the prospect.

Planning for objections

Specific strategies can help you respond constructively to each of the five types of objections. See each type of objection for information about how you can handle it.

"Happy with what we have"

You should respond to the "Happy with what we have" type of objection by finding out what the prospect currently has, determining how your offering is unique, and explaining how it could provide better value, given the prospect's existing or future needs. For example, you could start by asking "What benefits could we offer that you aren't currently receiving?" or "How are your needs likely to change over the next quarter or year?"

You might also uncover an opportunity to complement what a competitor is providing. For example, your company might be able to provide a prospect with 24-hour after-sales support, which an existing product supplier isn't currently providing.

"Not interested"

A good response to an objection of the "not interested" type is naming relevant companies that had similar objections until they found out how what you offer could really benefit them.

Similarly, you can ask prospects whether they've experienced a common problem in the industry and explain how your offering protects against or resolves this problem.

For example, you might say "You know, a lot of companies I've worked with said the same thing, until they found out just how much processing power this system frees up and how that improves network functioning."

"Too busy"

Often when prospects indicate they're too busy, they're simply resisting change. You could address this by asking what changes the prospect is currently facing and gaining agreement that they'll need to adapt.

If a prospect asks you to send details in the mail, you should focus on securing a face-to-face meeting instead. For example, you might respond with "There's a lot of information, so why don't we meet next Thursday at 11 a.m. and I'll take you through the most important aspects."

"Already have a supplier"

One of the most important aspects of responding to this type of objection is to avoid directly criticizing a prospect's current suppliers.

Instead, using third-party references where possible, you might offer to supplement what the prospect has. This will depend on your identifying a potential niche your company can fill. You can also include some key features of your offering if you know of any gaps these may fill.

"Price is too high"

If prospects argue that price is too high, you should agree that the price is high but then explain what value they'll receive as a result.

For example, you might say "I agree our service isn't the cheapest in the market, but it is one of the most cost-effective. This is because of the quality we offer and the levels of efficiency that result from our service."

Working through objections

Vincent, who works for a company that provides telecommunications solutions, is part-way through a cold call to Dawn, a potential client.

Follow along as Vincent handles Dawn's objections.

Dawn: Look I'm really busy. I don't have time for this. *Dawn is irritable and abrupt.*

Vincent: Yes. I completely understand. That's why I'd like to set up an appointment for next week if possible. Let me throw out a day and time – say next Tuesday at 3:30? *Vincent responds calmly and professionally.*

Dawn: What did you say you wanted to talk about? *Dawn is still irritable and suspicious.*

Vincent: Customizing telecommunications for your organization... *Dawn cuts across Vincent as he tries to explain.*

Dawn: Our system's fine. *Dawn responds in a dismissive tone.*

Vincent: That's great, but have you considered a voice-over-IP solution between branches? It's reduced telecommunications costs up to 30% for many of our clients – like Brocadero and the local hospital in your area. *Vincent replies patiently and with confidence.*

Dawn: Really? 30%? Hmm... When did you say you could come in, and how long would it take? *Dawn remains abrupt but concedes a point.*

Vincent successfully counters the "too busy" and "happy with what we have" objections that Dawn makes. He focuses on securing a meeting, finds a potential niche for his company, and backs up his claims using third-party references.

Question

Match the examples of cold-calling objections to suitable responses for overcoming them.

Options:

A. "We already have a software solution."

B. "We don't need additional customer support."

C. "Why don't you e-mail me the specs and I'll go through them when I have more time?"

D. "We're already working with your competition."

E. "We don't have the budget for that."

Targets:

1. "A unique feature of our company is that it provides 24×7 after-sales support."

2. "Our other clients have achieved marked increases in sales due to better customer satisfaction."

3. "I could drop off the information for you and answer any questions."

4. "OK. We could supplement that with our after-sales training."

5. "Other companies that switched to us report significant savings in resource use."

Answer:

The objection "We already have a software solution" fits in the "happy with what we have" category. A suitable response is to focus on something unique your company can provide, such as round-the-clock after-sales support.

The objection "We don't need additional customer support" fits in the "not interested" category. In this case, a suitable response is to explain the potential benefits of what you're offering – such as improved customer satisfaction and increased sales.

When a prospect asks for information to be e-mailed due to unavailable time, this objection falls in the "too busy" category. In this case, you should focus on securing a meeting – for example, by offering to drop off the information in person.

The objection that a prospect is already working with your competition fits in the "already have a supplier" category. To respond, you should focus on how you could complement the competitor's efforts – for example, by providing after-sales training.

The objection about lack of budget fits in the "price too high" category. The best response is to explain the value of your offering – for example, how it has resulted in significant savings or benefits for other companies.

The objections that a prospect may make during a cold call can generally be categorized into one of five types. Prospects may feel happy with what they already have, feel they don't need what you have to offer, already be working with the competition, feel too busy to explore the issue, or feel that your price will be too high.

You can use specific strategies to help overcome each type of objection.

MAKING A COLD CALL THAT LEADS TO AN APPOINTMENT

Making a cold call that leads to an appointment

During a cold call, you need to capture a prospect's attention. You do this by avoiding gimmicky openings, using the prospect's name in your greeting, and speaking politely and intelligently.

You motivate the prospect to answer questions by keeping the call short and conversational. You state your name and role, your company's name, and that you want to make an appointment. You should never talk fast, lie, or mislead the prospect in any way. You ask probing, open-ended questions that seek to match your product or service to the prospect's business needs.

To address any objections you adapt your response to the category the objection falls into – "happy with what we have," "not interested," "too busy," "already have a supplier," and "price too high."

CHAPTER II - QUALIFYING SALES PROSPECTS

CHAPTER II - Qualifying Sales Prospects

You need to find out their requirements so you have appropriate solutions to offer. When you take this kind of approach, it increases your chances of making a sale.

In this chapter, you'll learn what initial planning and research you should perform to qualify a prospect. You'll learn why it's important to conduct a qualification meeting and how to do this effectively. Finally, you'll learn how best to develop a lead you've qualified into a sales opportunity.

PLAN FOR A QUALIFYING MEETING

Plan for a qualifying meeting

What qualifying a prospect involves
Much of your time as a salesperson is spent contacting potential customers to introduce and sell your product or service. But many salespeople end up wasting a lot of their time on customers who are not interested in what they're selling. This reinforces the importance of qualifying prospects.

Qualifying involves finding out more about your prospects so you can differentiate between those who do and don't represent possible sales opportunities. To do this effectively, it's important to be able to distinguish between an inquiry, a lead, and a qualified sales lead.

See each term to find out more about it.
Inquiry
An inquiry is a request from someone for information about a product or service. The person requires some level of assistance. But not everyone who contacts you will be interested in what you're currently selling.

Lead

A lead is a potential customer who's interested in what you're selling.

For example, if you're a sales representative for a pharmaceutical company, a lead would be a doctor who is likely to prescribe the type of medication you're selling.

Qualified sales lead

A qualified sales lead is someone who's not only likely to be interested but is able and likely to go ahead with a purchase. This person may also be the source of profitable business opportunities and referrals in the future.

The qualified lead is someone who will have the attributes of your ideal customer profile, which describes the type of customer whose business problems your sales solution can help resolve.

If you're selling generic blood pressure medication, for example, your ideal customer profile might include hospital pharmacies. Your ideal customers should have a proven track record of selling generic medication and be aiming to provide their own customers with cost-effective health-care solutions.

Question

You're responsible for selling new payroll software. You have a list of human resources service providers who, based on their track records, are likely to be interested in this new product and able to purchase it.

Who are you describing?

Options:
1. Leads
2. Inquiries
3. Qualified leads

Answer:

Leads and those who've simply made inquiries about what you have to offer may be interested in your product, but you don't know that they're able and likely to purchase it. So in this case, you're describing qualified leads. You know that there's a good chance that they'll become your customers.

To secure qualified sales leads, you need to narrow the list of prospects you've identified to only those who offer real potential for a sale. This requires you to research your prospects. The more effectively you do this, the more you can target your sales efforts, and the more successful you'll be.

Researching your prospects

The process of identifying which prospects can be categorized as qualified sales leads has two phases. You complete a preliminary qualification phase when you place a cold call to a prospect.

During the call, you determine whether the prospect will fit an overall target profile. Ideally, you also get a general sense of whether the prospect can and will make a purchase, and identify the person responsible for making the final decision to buy.

During the detailed analysis phase, you investigate the prospect further. This involves conducting research to establish whether the prospect is a close enough match to your ideal customer profile to warrant further investigation.

It also involves developing objectives, along with a strategy, and an agenda for the eventual qualification meeting.

During the detailed analysis phase, you should get more information about your prospect:

- find out more about the industry the prospect is in – for example, find out what the latest innovations and the key challenges are,
- look up the prospect's annual revenue,
- confirm the size of the prospect's company based on total number of employees,
- determine the prospect's customer base, including where it operates – for example, locally or internationally – and
- research the prospect's corporate values and company culture.

As well as gathering more general information, you should aim to investigate a prospect's situation, goals, and business needs.

See each type of information to find out more about why it's important.

Situation

It's important to learn about a prospect's business situation.

For example, a pharmacy that's currently facing serious financial difficulties is unlikely to make a large purchase of new medication.

Goals

You need to know about a prospect's goals to establish whether the product or service you offer will help achieve those goals.

If a pharmacy wants to offer cheaper alternatives as a strategy for becoming more competitive, for example, you'll know that low-cost generic medication could help it achieve its goal.

Needs

A prospect has a business need whenever actual conditions fall short of those that are desired. Generally, the greater a prospect's need, the more likely it is that you'll make a sale. If you know about a need, you'll also be able to develop a convincing argument in favor of using your product or service.

For example, a pharmacy regularly runs out of generic medications because of increased demand. This alerts you to its need for an increased supply.

As part of your research on a prospect, you need to confirm who in the prospect's company will make the final decision about whether to purchase your product so you can tailor your sales pitch accordingly.

To sell medication to an executive, for example, you'll need to focus on how your product can increase sales and profits.

If the decision maker is a pharmacist, you might focus on your product's efficacy and lack of side effects.

You'll also need to be prepared to respond to objections when talking to a prospect. For example, if the prospect tells you that his pharmacy is already stocking a similar product, you need to be able to explain how the one you're offering differs and fills a specific need.

In addition, you'll want to support any claims you make about your product or service. The best way to do this is to collate research findings from reputable sources or testimonials.

As part of your preparation, you should ensure that you're able to explain why the prospect should choose you over your competitors. What makes the product or service you're offering unique? And how can it contribute to the prospect's own competitive edge?

You'll also want to establish the commitments you'd like from a qualified sales lead. For example, you might determine that at minimum, you'd like the prospect to agree to a trial period during which the popularity of your product is tested before a final sales agreement is drawn up.

And finally, you should plan to find out the prospect's success criteria, or the metrics the prospect will use to determine whether your product or service has met its objectives. This will help you establish whether your offering can meet the prospect's needs.

Question

Which steps should you take to research a prospect before a qualification meeting?

Options:

1. Determine the size and location of the prospect's operations
2. Discover any gap between what the prospect has and what they would like to have
3. Find out whether the prospect is considering expansion
4. Ask who has the authority to sign a sales agreement
5. Determine the wording of the sales contract
6. Contact a person you know at the prospect's company with a sales offer

Answer:

Option 1: This is a correct option. Knowing the prospect's size and location can help you determine whether the customer matches to the criteria you've identified in an ideal customer profile.

Option 2: This option is correct. You should try to uncover any business needs the prospect has. A need in this context can be defined as a gap between actual and desired conditions.

Option 3: This option is correct. You need to research a prospect's business situation. A company that wants to expand may be more likely to be interested in your product than a company that's cutting back.

Option 4: This is a correct option. As part of your research, you should determine who will be responsible for a final decision about whether to purchase the product or service you're selling. You can then tailor your sales pitch accordingly.

Option 5: This is an incorrect option. You're not yet ready to negotiate a sales contract. You're still determining whether the prospect matches your ideal customer profile.

Option 6: This option is incorrect. Qualifying a prospect involves investigating whether the prospect matches your ideal customer profile. It's premature to make a sales offer before doing this.

Preparing for a qualification meeting

Once you've completed your initial research, you should get ready for the actual qualification meeting by identifying your objectives, strategy, and agenda. It can be helpful to use a meeting worksheet to do this.

See each heading in an example meeting worksheet for more information about how to prepare for a qualification meeting.

My objective

In the objectives section of the worksheet, you should list your goals for the qualification meeting. Each goal should link to both your company's and your prospect's business objectives.

Based on your research, you know that a particular pharmacy is in a position to buy your generic blood pressure medication. You also know it's aiming to increase its orders of generic medications. Accordingly, you might plan to use the qualification meeting to find out how much of your product the pharmacy would initially need and what the chances are for increased orders.

These amounts should match to your company's business objective of securing on-going orders for its medication.

In the example meeting worksheet, the My objective section lists three objectives – determine the amount of initial order, determine future requirements, and confirm the pharmacy's business objective is in line with your company's business objective.

My strategy

You should develop a strategy for convincing the prospect of the value of meeting with you, as well as of the product or service you're offering.

For example, you might decide to e-mail a pharmacy a collection of research findings from reputable industry sources about the medication you're selling. You may plan to follow up with a call and a request to schedule a qualification meeting to discuss the findings, the pharmacy's requirements, and future developments in more detail.

The My strategy section of the worksheet specifies the strategies of e-mailing the prospect positive research findings from reputable sources about the generic, following up with a call to establish interest, and setting up a meeting to discuss details.

My agenda

The meeting agenda sets out the framework of the qualification meeting, or the questions you need to ask based on the research you've done. You should ensure that the agenda supports your business objectives for the meeting.

One of your objectives for a qualification meeting with a pharmacy is to identify the likely size of a possible order of generic blood pressure medication. So when planning the meeting's agenda, you prepare questions about the popularity of the generic medication the pharmacy currently stocks and about future trends.

The My agenda section lists several questions – How popular are your generic medications? What are some of the problems with the generic medications you stock? What are the deciding factors for stocking generic medication? Who are the people that decide which medication to stock? Do you stock any generic blood pressure medication and, if yes, which brand? and What future trends do you foresee in your use of generic medication?

Question

Which steps help you get ready for the actual qualification meeting with a prospect?

Options:

1. Consider why the meeting has value for the prospect
2. Know your goals for the meeting
3. Prepare the questions you want to ask

4. Work out a sales pitch that you can use with most prospects

5. Call a close contact to put in a good word for you

Answer:

Option 1: This option is correct. You need to develop a strategy that will convince your prospects that the meeting and the product you're selling will be of value to them.

Option 2: This is a correct option. You need to outline your objectives and link them to your and your prospect's company to create business value.

Option 3: This option is correct. You need to prepare your agenda, which consists of a set of questions, based on research, that you need to ask.

Option 4: This is an incorrect option. A generic sales pitch is likely to fail to convince your prospects because it doesn't consider their individual needs.

Option 5: This option is incorrect. You need to find out who the person with decision-making powers is and contact this person – not just any close contact.

A qualified sales lead is a prospect you've determined is able and likely to make a purchase. Qualifying prospects involves conducting research about them and clarifying how your product or service may address their business needs.

To prepare for a qualification meeting, you find out information about your prospect's company, including its revenue, size, customer base, and culture. You also determine your objectives for the meeting, along with a strategy and an agenda.

CONDUCTING A QUALIFICATION MEETING

Conducting a qualification meeting

Introducing the qualification meeting

During the preliminary qualification phase, which usually takes place through a cold call to a potential prospect, you determine whether the person is worth pursuing. If so, you set an appointment to further clarify the person's needs. Meeting face to face is usually more effective than a phone call for the detailed qualification meeting.

An effective qualification meeting includes two phases:
1. the opening, during which you build rapport, state your purpose, and get feedback, and
2. the time to ask questions, during which you aim to discover the needs of the prospect.

Guidelines for opening a meeting

Jason is responsible for selling an information management system designed specifically for operations managers in the oil and gas industry. He has conducted background research and scheduled a meeting with Luke, a prospect who's in charge of drilling operations at a national oil producer. Jason has run slightly late because of traffic, so he's keen to explain his product as soon as he sits down with Luke.

Follow along as Jason opens the qualification meeting with Luke.

Jason: Let's get straight to it. I'm offering an exceptional information system – it'll predict your daily output. *Jason is enthusiastic.*

Luke: Our software has advanced predictive capabilities already. So I'm not... *Luke is uninterested.*

Jason: But I'm sure what you have isn't as user friendly as this. Our interface is simple. Training will be minimal. Just look at these test results.

Luke: You know. This just isn't something we need right now. *Jason is a little desperate. He points at his laptop.*

Luke: You know. This just isn't something we need right now. *Luke is uninterested and closes a folder, putting an end to the meeting.*

Question

What do you think is the main element missing from Jason's opening?

Options:

1. He didn't build rapport with Luke

2. He didn't clearly explain why Luke's current system is ineffective

3. He forgot to summarize the benefits of his product

Answer:

Option 1: This is the correct option. One of the first things to do when you meet a prospect is to build rapport.

Option 2: This is an incorrect option. Beginning a meeting by explaining what's wrong with the prospect's current project is a surefire way to alienate the prospect.

Option 3: This option is incorrect. It's not effective to begin a qualification meeting by focusing on the benefits of your product. You need to relate the benefits to your prospect's needs.

To set the stage for an effective qualification meeting, you should open by following four steps. First build rapport with the prospect. This is something Jason failed to do. Then summarize your preparations for the meeting and clarify the purpose of the meeting. Finally, get feedback about whether your purpose matches your prospect's expectations.

See each step for more information about how to open effectively.

1. Build rapport

It's important to build rapport with the prospect so you can obtain the information you need and lay the foundation for a possible partnership.

You build rapport by projecting a positive and sincere image. You should dress professionally and be punctual. On arriving, greet your prospect and be prepared to exchange pleasantries for a few minutes, taking your lead from the prospect instead of doing all the talking.

You might talk about local issues or events. Or you might recount a funny incident that happened on your way to the meeting. But remember to avoid potentially sensitive subjects, such as religion and politics. And don't spend too long on this step either. Most people have busy schedules and like to get down to business as soon as possible.

2. Summarize preparations

You should briefly indicate how you've prepared for the meeting to make it clear you've given some thought to your prospect's circumstances. This is likely to make the prospect more receptive to your questions.

For example, you can get a prospect's attention by starting a sentence with "I've read through your company's annual report and I found..." or "After our previous call, I investigated the problems you raised and..."

3. Clarify purpose

Stating why you're having the meeting can help ensure that both you and the prospect have the same expectations. The purpose you specify should outline a benefit for the prospect, in the form of a business problem you may be able to help address.

For instance, you might say something like "I'd like to find out more about the supply chain issues you've been facing. Then we can investigate some possible solutions."

4. Get feedback

As a final step in opening the meeting, you should invite feedback from the prospect about the purpose of the meeting. This will help ensure that you both have the same expectations, and get the prospect talking.

For example, you could simply ask "Does that meet your expectations?"

Opening the qualification meeting

So how should Jason have opened the qualification meeting with Luke? He is meeting with Emily, another prospect in the oil drilling industry. This time he makes sure he is on time. Punctuality is important if you're to succeed in building rapport with a prospect.

Follow along as Jason opens the qualification meeting with Emily.

Jason: Morning Emily. I see the new bridge is finished. *Jason is cheerful.*

Emily: Yes. You're lucky you didn't come here before the bridge – traffic was awful. Do you want to get started? You mentioned a new reporting tool over the phone. *Emily is enthusiastic.*

Jason: That's right. But I'd like to find out what you need first. So I can understand how exactly my product can help. How does that sound? *Jason is enthusiastic.*

Emily: Sounds good. I'd also like to discuss some of the mobile solutions you're offering. *Emily is willing to talk.*

Question

How does Jason appropriately open this meeting with Emily?

Options:

1. He starts by building rapport
2. He summarizes his preparations for the meeting
3. He clarifies the meeting's purpose
4. He asks Emily if she agrees with his statements about the meeting's purpose
5. He focuses his attention on his product's advantages

Answer:

Option 1: This is a correct option. Jason builds rapport with Emily by being punctual and then exchanging pleasantries. This relaxes both parties and makes it more likely that the prospect will share information openly.

Option 2: This option is incorrect. Jason fails to summarize his preparations. This can be an important part of any opening because it can show a prospect the salesperson has thought about a customer and isn't only interested in making a sale.

Option 3: This is a correct option. Jason clarifies the purpose so both parties have the same expectations.

Option 4: This is a correct option. Jason was right to ask Emily for feedback after outlining the purpose of the meeting. He can then check that both he and Emily have the same expectations.

Option 5: This option is incorrect. Jason opens the meeting by engaging with Emily, not overwhelming her with talk about his product.

Guidelines for asking questions

After a brief opening in which you establish rapport and state your purpose, you're going to want to ask your prospect some questions. It helps to group your questions according to certain qualification criteria – for example, the prospect's current business environment, the business needs and problems your prospect faces, and your prospect's competition.

Grouping questions helps you structure the meeting and avoid unnecessary confusion. You can use other criteria as well:

- the prospect's decision-making processes and criteria, or the means by which decisions are made in the prospect's company,
- your prospect's time frame for addressing a specified business need, and
- your prospect's budget, to help you determine the extent of the solution you can offer.

Although you may group your questions into categories to help structure your session with a prospect, it's also important to be flexible and respond to what the prospect says. Try to be conversational. Other guidelines to follow when asking questions are to use an effective style, know which types of questions to avoid, and, above all, listen.

To order questions so that the discussion flows logically, you need to listen carefully to each of a prospect's answers, and formulate your next question based on that answer.

For example, you ask a prospect about what they value most in a supplier, and the prospect tells you – prompt deliveries. You respond by saying something about your delivery record before asking the prospect to elaborate on scheduling.

Question

In response to a question about what your prospect's main problem is, your prospect tells you that current suppliers don't have enough stock.

What is the most appropriate question to ask next?

Options:

1. "Which products run out of stock most often?"

2. "By when will you have decided on the new supplier?"

3. "How far do your suppliers have to travel to deliver your goods?"

Answer:

You should ask questions that follow on logically from your prospect's answer. Asking about when a decision about new suppliers will be made and how far other suppliers need to travel has very little to do with the fact that the prospect doesn't have enough stock.

It's also important to be conversational in tone. This helps put your prospect at ease. And dialog flows better when people feel comfortable. Being conversational means using short sentences, and shorter words than you might in a more formal situation. You'll want to use contractions and words that are in common usage and more immediately understandable – for example, use "but" instead of "notwithstanding" or "list" instead of "enumerate." Finally, use the active voice. It often sounds more natural.

In addition to the other guidelines, using an appropriate questioning style will help you get the information you need. This involves making effective use of open-ended, close-ended, and indirect questions.

See each question type to find out more about its appropriate use.

Open-ended

You use open-ended question to elicit full responses, which prospects are free to put in their own words. Generally about 80% of your questions should be open-ended.

These types of questions usually start with words like "Why" or "What." An example is "What capabilities do you need from this tool?"

Close-ended

You use close-ended questions to elicit short responses, like "Yes" or "No." Close-ended questions often start with "When," "Who," "Where," "How much," or "Have you." They're useful for bringing a conversation back on track, confirming what a prospect has said, or obtaining highly specific information.

"How much are you willing to pay for the upgrade?" and "Have you heard about the latest development in data analysis technology?" are examples of close-ended questions.

Indirect

An indirect question consists of a polite expression followed by the actual question. For example, the direct question "What budget have you set aside for this project?" becomes "Can you tell me what budget you've set aside for this project?"

By adding "Can you tell me," you've made the question less threatening and you're therefore more likely to receive an answer. You can also add an introductory phrase such as "I wonder" or "I'd like to know." This improves the conversational tone as well.

There are some question styles you'll want to avoid during a qualification meeting – namely, an interrogative style. This involves asking multiple questions, one after the other, without giving the prospect a chance to answer fully or elaborate. This style is intimidating and unlikely to get you the detailed answers you need.

Your question style shouldn't be apologetic. For example, avoid starting your questions with "I wish I didn't have to ask, but..." or "I'm sorry, but do you..." Instead you need to appear confident, or you may not be seen as trustworthy.

You should also avoid leading questions, which suggest possible answers. For example, you should rephrase the question "Speed and accuracy are important features in a reporting tool, aren't they?" as "What reporting tool features are important to you?"

As an overall guideline, practice active listening. You should focus your attention on what the prospect says, avoid interrupting, and ask for clarification if you don't understand something.

To make it clear you are listening, you can take notes.

It also helps to summarize what the prospect has said in your own words to demonstrate that you were listening, check your understanding, and strengthen the prospect's recognition of the identified business needs.

When you summarize what the prospect has said, you might start with a simple lead-in such as "So what we've discussed so far is..."

You should then get feedback from the prospect, confirming you've understood correctly. For example, you can ask "Have I summarized your company's needs correctly?"

Once you've got confirmation, you can proceed to discuss possible solutions to the prospect's expressed needs. You want to be specific here – rather than stating general solutions you have found to work with other companies, you need to offer specific solutions for each prospect. This shows you are listening and taking an active interest.

Question

Which guidelines can help you ask questions effectively during a qualification meeting?

Options:

1. Ask questions that prompt the prospect to elaborate fully.

2. Group related questions, such as those related to the prospect's current business situation.

Essential Selling Skills

3. Avoid questions like "I guess reliability is the most important criterion for you when choosing a supplier – is that right?"

4. Avoid using an overly formal tone.

5. Ask the most important questions, which relate to the prospect's budget, first.

6. Lead into questions by using wording like "I hate having to ask you this, but...?"

Answer:

Option 1: This option is correct. You should use mostly open-ended questions during qualification meetings to encourage prospects to provide full responses in their own words.

Option 2: This is a correct option. You should group related questions to help structure the meeting and keep it focused.

Option 3: This option is correct because this is an example of a leading question. It supplies an expected answer and so limits the prospect's likely response.

Option 4: This is a correct option. You should aim to be conversational, rather than overly stiff or formal to keep the prospect at ease and ready to talk openly.

Option 5: This is an incorrect option. It's important to order your questions so they flow logically and lead on from your prospect's answers. For example, you'd probably ask about the prospect's budget only after asking about the business needs that the prospect wants to address.

Option 6: This is an incorrect option. Starting a question with "I hate having to ask you this, but..." is apologetic and indicates a lack of confidence.

Asking questions

Jason opened the qualification meeting with Emily successfully. He's now able to ask the questions that will let him discover whether Emily is a qualified sales lead.

Follow along as Jason asks questions to discover more about the needs of Emily's company.

Jason: So your current reporting tool – which software does it run?

Emily: Phlogistix CTA.

Jason: I know that module. It was our top seller a while back. What other capabilities do you need? Beyond what this tool gives you?

Emily: Well, the trend analysis capability is outdated. It logs a lot of data, but it's tough to analyze. I waste a day a month filtering data.

Jason: So you'd like a tool with filtering capabilities? How important is it for the tool to display return on investments based on the filtered data?

Emily: Very important. That type of information can link what's happening onsite to our business objectives.

Jason follows the guidelines for asking questions. He uses open-ended questions, which allow Emily to respond in full, according to her own experiences.

He listens to Emily's responses and asks questions that follow logically from what she says.

Benefits of a qualification meeting

Conducting an effective qualification meeting can result in several benefits.

Question

What do you think are some of the benefits of conducting an effective qualification meeting?

Essential Selling Skills

Options:
1. You build trust and credibility
2. You can match your sales pitch to a prospect's needs
3. You can identify prospects who have a need and are willing to buy from you
4. You can determine the prospect's annual revenue
5. You will be able to finalize a sale

Answer:

Conducting an effective meeting doesn't necessarily help you to determine a prospect's annual revenue or enable you to finalize a sale. It helps you build trust and credibility, enables you to match your pitch to needs, and enables you to check whether your prospect is willing to buy.

The benefits of being able to conduct an effective qualification meeting are that you can build trust and credibility with the prospect, you'll be in a better position to match your sales pitch to the prospect's needs, and you can confirm whether a prospect represents a legitimate sales opportunity.

Once you've identified a qualified sales lead and have a good understanding of the prospect's business needs, you're equipped to make an effective sales offer.

Case Study: Question 1 of 2

Scenario

Kevin is a salesperson for a manufacturer of household cleaners. He's meeting with Taku, the manager for housekeeping at a national hotel chain, to establish if Taku's company is a qualified sales lead.

Answer the questions about how Kevin conducts the meeting in the given order.

Question

What does Kevin do appropriately during the qualification meeting?

Options:

1. He's on time and starts by exchanging pleasantries with Taku
2. He summarizes his preparations for the meeting
3. He clarifies the purpose of the meeting
4. He uses open-ended and indirect questions
5. He controls the speed of the meeting by asking many close-ended questions that are easy to answer
6. He doesn't waste time repeating what the prospect has said before moving on to discuss possible solutions

Answer:

Option 1: This is a correct option. Kevin builds rapport with Taku by being on time and by discussing news that may be of interest to Taku. This makes Taku feel more comfortable.

Option 2: This option is correct. By summarizing his preparations for the meeting, Kevin shows he's thought about the prospect's circumstances and needs. Taku may feel more inclined to listen to him because of this.

Option 3: This is a correct option. Kevin clarifies the purpose of the meeting to ensure that his and the prospect's expectations are the same.

Option 4: This is a correct option. Kevin uses mainly open-ended questions at the start of the meeting to encourage Taku to answer fully and in his own words. When Kevin has to ask a sensitive question about the prospect's budget, he uses an indirect question.

Option 5: This is an incorrect option. Kevin shouldn't interrogate Taku, asking multiple questions one after the other. Also, he should use close-ended questions to control the content of the conversation, not its speed.

Option 6: This option is incorrect. It's important to listen actively during a qualification meeting. One characteristic of active listening is summarizing what the other person has said to confirm understanding before moving on. Moreover, Kevin needs to propose specific solutions, rather than general ones, for Taku's needs.

Case Study: Question 2 of 2

How could Kevin improve the way he conducts the meeting?

Options:

1. He should ask Taku for feedback about the purpose of the meeting

2. He should listen more actively by making notes

3. He should let Taku finish speaking before responding to him

4. He should be more apologetic when asking about the prospect's budget

5. He should ask more close-ended questions than open-ended ones

Answer:

Option 1: This is a correct option. Kevin should have confirmed that Taku agrees with the purpose he outlined for the meeting.

Option 2: This option is correct. Kevin should practice active listening. He didn't do enough to show that he was interested or to encourage Taku to provide him with more information.

Option 3: This is a correct option. Kevin should practice his active listening skills and not interrupt Taku.

Option 4: This is an incorrect option. It's important to come across as confident, rather than apologetic, during a qualification meeting.

Option 5: This option is incorrect. Kevin should stick mostly to open-ended questions to get Taku talking about his needs. Close-ended questions can be used too – to clarify something or move the conversation along.

To open a qualification meeting effectively, you need to build rapport, summarize your preparations for the meeting, clarify the meeting's purpose, and get feedback.

You then need to ask questions. You should group related questions based on established qualification criteria, use an effective questioning style and know which types of questions to avoid, and remain conversational. You should also order your questions based on the prospect's responses and listen actively.

The benefits of a qualification meeting are that it helps you to build trust and credibility, match your sales message to a prospect's needs, and determine whether the prospect represents a sales opportunity.

STEPS TO QUALIFY A PROSPECT

Steps to qualify a prospect

Preparing for a qualification meeting

Determining whether a prospect really represents a sales opportunity is important. To do this, you conduct some initial research, including calling the prospect and setting up an appointment if they seem like a likely match for what you are selling. Then you prepare for a more detailed qualification meeting. Your aim is to further investigate the prospect's needs and how these could be addressed by what you're selling.

Conducting an effective qualification meeting involves two main steps:
1. controlling the opening, during which you should build rapport, summarize your preparations for the meeting, state the purpose of the meeting, and get feedback, and
2. asking the right questions to obtain the information you need from your prospect.

Conducting the meeting

An opening that builds rapport, summarizes your preparations, clarifies your purpose, and gets feedback for the purpose will set the stage for an effective qualification meeting.

To ask questions that give you the answers you need, you apply effective question styles; avoid interrogating, apologetic, and leading questions; maintain a conversational tone; formulate questions that logically follow on from the answers you get; and be an active listener.

TRANSFORM A QUALIFIED LEAD INTO A SALES OPPORTUNITY

Transform a qualified lead into a sales opportunity

To qualify a sales lead, you need to research and discuss a prospect's business requirements in detail. Once you've done this, the next step is to develop the qualified sales lead into a sales opportunity, by proposing possible solutions to the prospect's needs.

Consider Jennifer, a salesperson for a supply chain solutions company. She has identified Silvia's global transportation company as a qualified sales lead. Silvia, the logistics manager, wants clients to be able to track goods online, in real time. Jennifer decides to meet with Silvia to propose a possible solution.

Follow along as Jennifer meets with Silvia to discuss solutions.

Jennifer: Silvia, did you know we set up a call center for Brocadero. They love it. *Jennifer is eager to impress.*

Silvia: But we don't want to work with a call center. Our clients want to track their goods themselves, online. *Silvia shakes her head when she speaks about not wanting to work with a call center.*

Jennifer: I understand but the call center offers 24-hour service. It's much easier – someone does the work for you. *Jennifer continues to sell her solution.*

Silvia: It's not really what we want... *Silvia rejects Jennifer's solutions.*

Jennifer's mistake

Jennifer failed to base the solution she offered on Silvia's needs, which she should have identified during a qualification meeting. Instead she based her offer on what worked well for another client. As a result, Jennifer may lose the sale.

Developing solution objectives

The best way to develop a qualified sales lead into a sales opportunity is to follow a three-step process. Develop solution objectives, explore potential solutions, and finally agree on a solution.

First you need to revisit the needs expressed during the qualification meeting and then break each need down into solution objectives. These define what should change for the prospect as a result of the solution you provide. For example, a client might want to be able to process 150 orders per hour. Solution objectives should be specific, measurable, attainable, and complementary.

See each characteristic of effective solution objectives for more information about it.

Specific

Solution objectives should be specific so it's clear what the solution should achieve. An example of a specific solution objective is to deliver 99.5% of goods on time.

Measurable

A solution objective must be measurable so you can determine whether it's being met. For example, a measurable solution objective is to increase customer satisfaction by 2%.

Attainable

All solution objectives need to be attainable if you're to meet a prospect's needs. You should propose a solution only if you can implement it.

Complementary

You may break down a need into multiple solution objectives. These should complement one another.

For example, a call center wants to increase customer satisfaction, so its solution objectives are to decrease call times and increase data accuracy. If your solution can achieve both objectives, the objectives complement each other.

Exploring potential solutions

Based on the objectives you develop, you can explore potential solutions. It's important that you and the prospect work together at this point, to ensure that each solution you consider will meet the prospect's needs.

You need to link each solution objective to a potential solution. For example, you might need to find the appropriate database technology to meet a call center's objective of decreasing call times.

You also need to identify criteria for measuring whether a possible solution meets the relevant need. For instance, the database technology should help customer service representatives answer, resolve, and log calls within an average of three minutes per call.

When exploring solutions for a prospect, you want to try to match a benefit of what you can provide to a need the prospect has. To find that match, you should outline one potential benefit of your product or service for the prospect at a time.

Ask the prospect for feedback about each benefit you identify, working together and exploring the options fully.

You do this until you're sure the prospect likes a solution you've explored.

Agreeing on a solution

The final step is to agree on a solution. This involves securing an agreement that what you're proposing will meet a prospect's needs. This is crucial because once you have this agreement, you're almost guaranteed a sale. To facilitate the process, you need to keep the prospect engaged and be able to support your claims.

See each method to find out more about it.

Keep the prospect engaged

You can use various methods to keep the prospect engaged. One way to do this is to ask for feedback. For example, you might ask "Is this the type of result you need?" to draw the prospect into discussion.

Another method is using phrasing to imply the prospect already owns your product – as in "Your production line will record an immediate drop in defects." Also use "we" to create a sense that you're working together to find a solution.

Some prospects like to see a product you're selling, so take it with you if possible. If you have samples, give them to the prospect, who may then distribute them to other interested parties.

Support your claims

You need to appear credible throughout your discussions, so provide evidence for the claims you make. Possible sources are customer satisfaction surveys, industry survey data, and reviews from trade magazines or reputable specialists in your field.

Offer a guarantee that you'll work with the prospect until the solution delivers on your promises.

Developing a qualified sales opportunity

Recall Jennifer, a salesperson for a supply chain solutions company, who failed to match her solution to the needs of Silvia's transportation company. Jennifer gets a second chance to develop Silvia into a sales opportunity.

Follow along as Jennifer proposes a solution to Silvia.

Jennifer: So your clients want to track their goods online in real time? And you want to increase your customer numbers by 5% a year after you've introduced this tool?

Silvia: That's right. Our Marketing Department tells us we need it. To keep up with industry trends.

Jennifer: Our latest tracking software can offer the real-time environment you're looking for.

Silvia: What tests have been run on it?

Jennifer: It's been tested and approved by a number of leading logistics companies. And you'll be able to easily integrate the tracking software into your existing IT infrastructure. There's also a monitoring system that's simple to use. What do you think?

Silvia: I like what you're proposing. Could you demonstrate it for me in a test environment?

Jennifer: Of course, why don't we agree on a date?

Jennifer develops solution objectives by stating Silvia's need for a tracking tool. She then breaks the need down into a solution objective, which is to increase the number of customers by 5% within a year of introducing the tracking tool.

Jennifer explores a potential solution – her company's tracking tool. She outlines its benefits, including its real-time functionality, easy integration, and the monitoring system. She uses language that implies Silvia already owns the solution she's proposing. Silvia responds favorably to the proposed solutions.

Jennifer gets Silvia to agree to the solution, and Silvia asks for a demonstration.

Question

What steps do you take to develop a qualified lead into a sales opportunity?

Options:

1. Break down the needs expressed during the qualification meeting into objectives that define a solution's results

2. Match the solution's benefit to your prospect to a need

3. Ask your prospect for feedback about each benefit

4. Outline your research into the prospect's buying habits

5. Confirm that the person you're talking to can agree to make a purchase

Answer:

Option 1: This option is correct. You break each expressed need down into solution objectives that are specific, measurable, attainable, and complementary.

Option 2: This is a correct option. You should match each benefit the solution may have for the prospect to a need. You outline one benefit at a time and get feedback on each until you have your prospect's commitment.

Option 3: This option is correct. You should keep the prospect engaged by asking for feedback and by being able to support your claims about the benefits of the solution.

Option 4: This is an incorrect option. You should research your prospect before the qualification meeting and mention it in the opening to build rapport.

Option 5: This option is incorrect. You should establish the decision maker well before proposing a solution.

Developing a qualified sales lead into a sales opportunity involves matching what you can provide to a prospect's business needs. To do this, you can follow a process with three steps.

The first step is to develop solution objectives that are specific, measurable, attainable, and complementary. The second step is to explore potential solutions for achieving each objective, outlining the benefits that the solutions can provide and obtaining the prospect's feedback about these. The final step is to secure the prospect's agreement on a solution. To do this, you need to keep the prospect engaged and support your claims.

CHAPTER III - CLOSING THE SALE

CHAPTER III - Closing the Sale

In this chapter, you'll learn essential principles for closing a sale:
- how to develop a strong and effective value proposition,
- how to recognize when a prospect is ready to close based on the signs the prospect gives you,
- how to deal with sales objections appropriately,
- which key strategies you can use to close a sale, and
- how to follow up with the customer after the sale is complete.
-

STRONG VALUE PROPOSITIONS

Strong value propositions

The value proposition

From the very start of the sales process, your goal is to convince prospects that you can provide something of value to them. Your focus is on getting prospects to purchase your products or services.

After you've opened a sales call, qualified a sales lead, and made your presentation, you need to close the sale by getting a prospect's commitment to buy.

You shouldn't think of this as a separate effort. It should flow naturally from the preceding sales presentation and discussion.

Throughout the process, it's important not to focus just on making a sale. You should respect your prospects and aim to provide them with products or services that will help bring them success.

This makes it more likely your sales efforts will succeed.

It can also help you develop valuable, long-term relationships that generate multiple sales over time.

To close a sale and encourage a customer to engage with you again in the future, you need to provide the customer with an attractive value proposition.

A value proposition identifies the value, or benefits, a prospect can gain from your products or services.

It shouldn't include empty claims. Instead it should provide the prospect with relevant facts, figures, and compelling examples.

The value you can offer a prospect may be derived from different sources, including your product or service, your organization, you as the salesperson, and a short-term incentive.

See each source of value for more information about how to develop an effective value proposition.

Your product or service

Instead of just providing prospects with product specifications or service details, you need to link your offering to proven benefits for the prospects. So focus on telling prospects how your product or service has performed successfully in situations similar to theirs.

Your organization

If your organization has a good reputation and a history of success, these are essential selling points that you should take advantage of in your value proposition. You should also discuss your organization's vision and mission, core values, partnerships, and innovative initiatives.

Provide real examples rather than just making claims. For example, don't over-use buzz words like "loyalty" and "quality" to describe your organization. Instead, describe actions your organization takes that embody those qualities.

You

It's essential that prospects trust you and believe that you have their best interests in mind. To build this trust, you need to demonstrate your value. This could come in many forms, such as your industry knowledge, product knowledge, reliability, and understanding of the prospect's business needs.

Once prospects see you as a consultant rather than just a salesperson, you become a trusted advisor – which makes sales easier to close.

Short-term incentive

Short-term incentives are additional benefits you offer prospects provided they agree to conclude purchases. For example, you might offer a prospect additional units of a product for free, on condition that the prospect signs a purchase agreement within the next three days.

The understanding is that the value of the deal for the prospect will be lower in the future than it is now. This can encourage a sense of urgency, making it more likely a prospect will conclude a purchase.

When value propositions fail, it's generally because they're ineffective in presenting benefits. These propositions may include exaggerated claims or only provide descriptions of an organization's offerings.

See each type of problem for examples.

Exaggerated claims

An investment company could claim to offer "incredible performance in volatile markets." A retailer might say that it gives customers "the best prices on superior quality products." And a software development house may claim to use "best-of-breed, cutting-edge technologies to build the most robust, versatile systems in the world."

All of these claims use impressive phrases, but none give any practical, measurable metrics for the claims. The result is the propositions sound like nothing more than boastful marketing talk.

Descriptions of offerings

A training institute may say that it offers "a wide range of courses in various business areas." A furniture company might state that it sells "wooden, melamine, and plastic chairs, desks, and other furniture for the office environment." A research institute might say that its work involves conducting "focus groups and customer interviews to gauge public opinion of your business and products."

All these statements specify what each company sells, but they do nothing more than describe the offerings – making the value propositions sound boring and unattractive.

A strong, effective value proposition focuses on the tangible results a prospect could gain. Examples are reduced costs, higher profits, and increased customer retention. It also clearly links the benefits of a product or service to the prospect's unique business needs and challenges.

For example, say you're on the sales team for a technology company that develops internal components for cell phones and devices. Your customer is a cell phone manufacturer that needs to improve sales, and wants to do this by offering its own customers benefits that its competitors aren't.

You present a value proposition that centers around "innovative technology that boosts cell phone battery life by 60% and doubles phone storage capacity, as compared to the industry average."

Meeting customer needs

Natasha, the operations manager for a major healthcare group, has been tasked with bringing down operating costs for the coming year. She's meeting with Peggy, a sales executive from a document management and workflow software solutions company. Peggy has already made her presentation to Natasha, explaining the details of the document management solution, and is now eager to make the sale.

Follow along as Peggy tries to close the sale.

Peggy: So as you can see, our excellent service speaks for itself. *Peggy is optimistic.*

Natasha: Peggy, your track record is great, but I'm not sure about this document solution... *Natasha is skeptical.*

Peggy: What do you mean? *Peggy is confused.*

Natasha: Have you been listening? Service is important, sure, but I need to bring costs down. I don't see how your system is going to do that. *Natasha is doubtful.*

Peggy: Natasha, trust me, other customers also had reservations at first. But once they started using it, they were delighted they went with our solution. *Peggy is persistent.*

Natasha: This isn't about reservations – you haven't told me how this is going to save us money. *Natasha is concerned and unconvinced. Peggy is disappointed.*

In this scenario, Peggy missed the sale because she didn't give Natasha an effective value proposition. Peggy focused on her company's reputation and on other customers' reactions to her offering.

As a result, Natasha – whose focus is on addressing her own company's need to cut costs – was unconvinced and decided not to purchase the document management solution.

If you want to make a sale, you need to align your value proposition with what's most important to a prospect. So you need to customize your proposition to the prospect's unique situation and needs.

For example, Natasha's main need was to reduce her company's operating costs.

So Peggy should have focused her value proposition on exactly how her company's document management solution could cut the healthcare group's administration and communication costs.

Question

A software developer is trying to sell an inventory management system to a leading retailer, who's struggling to track and manage stock efficiently.

What are examples of strong value propositions?

Options:

1. "The system offers numerous features, such as stock tracking, audit trails, smart scanning, and customized reports."

2. "Our system reduces stock management overheads by 30%, and delivers 50% improved efficiency in inventory handling."

3. "Using state-of-the-art labeling and tracking technology, the program increases stock security and maximizes stock availability."

4. "Our award-winning, top-of-the-line technology provides superb usability and an engaging user interface."
Answer:
Option 1: This is an incorrect option. This value proposition simply describes some of the product's features. It doesn't make it clear how those features could be of value to the prospect.

Option 2: This option is correct. This value proposition outlines tangible results that the prospect can expect from the product. Using metrics, the proposition makes it clear how the product can be of value to the prospect.

Option 3: This is a correct option. This value proposition clearly outlines benefits that the prospect can realize by using the product.

Option 4: This option is incorrect. This value proposition is full of exaggerated claims but doesn't tell the prospect what tangible benefits the product can deliver.

SIGNS THAT YOUR PROSPECT IS READY TO CLOSE

Signs that your prospect is ready to close

Timing your closing

You also need to get your timing right if you're to close a sale. If prospects are still unsure or have objections, you need to resolve their concerns before attempting to close. And once prospects are already convinced to buy, there's no need to keep selling.

But how do you know when the time is right? You need to be able to read the signs that a prospect is ready to make a purchase. These signs relate to the pace of the conversation, questions prospects ask you, and the verbal cues the prospect provides.

See each sign of readiness for more information about it.

Pace

A change of pace in conversation usually signifies that prospects have made up their minds. If the pace has been relatively calm and a prospect then speeds up the conversation, it often indicates that the prospect is excited to push ahead and make a purchase.

If the pace has been normal and a prospect slows it down, it's likely that the prospect is making a final analysis of whether or not to proceed with a purchase.

Questions

When prospects start asking lots of specific questions, it usually means they're considering a purchase. As a result, they want to know more about issues that concern them.

For example, they may ask about your offering's quality, warranties, user instructions, safety, and other specific features. They might also ask for details associated with a possible purchase agreement, such as price, discounts, delivery schedule, and stock availability.

Verbal cues

When prospects start speaking positively about you or your company, it indicates that they trust your ability to solve their problems with your offering.

Take note of agreeable phrases that prospects may start using, such as "that sounds good," "that's interesting," or "that sounds like a good deal" – all of which may indicate a willingness to close the deal.

Question

What signs indicate that a prospect is ready to make a purchase?

Options:

1. The prospect speeds up the conversation

2. The prospect expresses doubt about your product's longevity

3. The prospect tells you that your deal seems like good value

4. The prospect reiterates the problems that his company is having

5. The prospect asks about stock availability and how quickly you can deliver

Answer:

Option 1: This option is correct. A change of pace usually signifies that prospects have made up their minds. A quicker pace typically indicates excitement and an eagerness to close the deal.

Option 2: This is an incorrect option. Negative sentiments about your product indicate that a sale is in jeopardy.

Option 3: This is a correct option. When prospects make positive comments, it suggests that they trust your ability to solve their problems with your offering.

Option 4: This option is incorrect. If prospects revert the focus to their own problems, it suggests you haven't succeeded in convincing them that your offering can meet their needs. So they're not ready to close at this point.

Option 5: This option is correct. Specific questions like this suggest that prospects are seriously considering a purchase.

To close a sale, you need to provide a prospect with an attractive value proposition. This should specify the tangible benefits your offering can have for the prospect. It should also relate these benefits to the prospect's unique business needs.

To close effectively, you also need to get your timing right. To do this, you have to be able to read the signs that a prospect is ready for you to close. For example, the prospect may change the pace of the conversation, ask specific questions, and make positive comments.

DEALING WITH SALES OBJECTIONS

Dealing with sales objections

Dealing with objections

In most sales situations, prospects are likely to raise objections to the propositions you make. In fact, there are times when all you seem to get are objections. Knowing how to handle these objections can be the difference between closing sales and losing sales.

Objections can be a positive sign. Consider that most objections are actually just questions or concerns in disguise. If they're voiced, it means you've been given an opportunity to respond.

As general guidelines for handling objections, you should retain a professional demeanor, always be polite, never take sales objections personally, and remain optimistic.

Also, never react instantly or defensively to an objection. Ensure you fully understand the prospect's concern and provide a considered response.

A good general process for dealing with objections includes five steps – listen, question, restate, empathize, and then resolve the objection.

See each step to learn more about it.

1. Listen

You should listen carefully and avoid interrupting when a prospect is making an objection. Also note any nonverbal signs that add to what the prospect is communicating.

2. Question

After listening to a prospect's objection, you should ask questions to ensure you've fully understood the prospect's concern and its causes. For example, if an objection relates to delivery dates, you might ask "How much time do you have before you need results?"

3. Restate

Once the prospect has explained an objection, you should confirm your understanding by restating what the prospect said in your own words and asking the prospect if this is correct.

4. Empathize

Once you've understood a prospect's objection, you should empathize with the prospect. Don't agree or disagree with what the prospect has said. Instead, acknowledge the prospect's concern and express a desire to resolve the issue.

5. Resolve the objection

After empathizing with the prospect, you should isolate the objection. This involves determining whether it's the only issue preventing the sale. If the prospect has other objections, you'll need to deal with them one by one in a similar way.

You should also validate the objection, determining whether it poses a legitimate problem. If the objection doesn't appear valid, you can explain your reasoning and reassure the prospect. Alternatively, you may focus on convincing the prospect that your product or service's advantages outweigh the problem posed in the objection.

Question

Jim is trying to sell an internal billing system to Natasha, a manager for a multinational company. To deal with the objection, Jim listens closely as Natasha expresses doubt about the time it will take the system to generate savings.

Match each remaining step of the process for handling objections to Jim's statement that exemplifies it.

Options:

A. Question
B. Restate
C. Empathize
D. Resolve the objection

Targets:

1. "What kind of payback period would you hope for?"

2. "So you're saying the system might not result in improvements fast enough to meet your company's needs?"

3. "It's tough when you're expected to get instant results, but I'm confident we can find a solution together."

4. "The savings are always instant. In fact, a cost-benefit analysis can show you'll recoup the money in just one year."

Answer:

Jim tries to understand the objection by clarifying the core aspect of Natasha's concern – the period of time it should take for the investment to show results.

Jim paraphrases the core issue and asks Natasha to confirm that his understanding is correct.

Jim empathizes with Natasha's difficulty and remains constructive by suggesting that a mutually acceptable solution is still possible.

Jim resolves the objection by assuring Natasha that the payback period will be relatively short, based on past experience and a mathematical analysis.

Countering a price objection

You'll encounter a wide range of objections when trying to close sales. For example, prospects may have concerns about a product's design, your ability to meet a delivery deadline, or the after-sales service you can provide. Perhaps the most common type of objection you should prepare for, however, is about price.

Often, price is the most obvious way for prospects to compare your offerings to those of your competitors. So to prepare for price objections, you should establish what differentiates your offering from others, which may be similar in price. For example, you might remind the prospect about your company's superior after-sales service.

Also, prepare to justify the price you're asking. To do this, focus on the monetary value your offering could have for a prospect, in relation to its price.

You'll then be equipped to present a strong and logical argument against any price objection, without appearing defensive or aggressive.

Bhadrak, who sells information management solutions, is meeting with Joe, the procurement manager for a major construction company. He knows that Joe's company has been seeking ways to improve communication between the various parties involved in its projects, such as architects, contractors, surveyors, inspectors, and project supervisors.

Follow along as the sales meeting proceeds.

Joe: Your solution sounds great, but ninety-five thousand? I'm getting prices from other vendors a lot lower than that. *Joe is skeptical.*

Bhadrak: So you don't have budget for a full solution? *Bhadrak is positive.*

Joe: Not a question of budget. Your price isn't competitive.

Bhadrak: But the other offers are for an off-the-shelf product, isn't that right? *Bhadrak is concluding.*

Joe: Yes. *Joe is agreeable.*

Bhadrak: Joe, how is off-the-shelf software going to give you what you need? What we're offering is an entire intranet portal customized to your company. *Bhadrak is empathetic.*

Bhadrak: We've reviewed the workflow issues. The communication headaches. Our solution is the only one that's going to deal with these. Within the year, it will save you money. *Bhadrak is empathetic and optimistic.*

Joe: OK...I can see how that might be the case. *Joe is enthusiastic.*

Bhadrak successfully dealt with Joe's price objection and made Joe comfortable enough to proceed with the sales process.

Bhadrak listened to Joe's argument – letting him explain – and then got clarification on the price issue.

He then confirmed the underlying issues, empathized with Joe, and refocused the discussion on the benefits of the solution. This helped isolate the price issue and justify the price of the system.

Case Study: Question 1 of 2
Scenario

Adam, who represents a software developer, is trying to sell his company's latest inventory management system to Charles, the managing director of a leading retailer.

Question

Given the conversation so far, what is it most appropriate for Adam to say next?

Options:

1. "I'm so sorry about that. I'll try to pull up the call details and see why the support was so poor."

2. "On average, how long did it take to resolve those calls? Hours? Or more than a day in most cases?"

3. "So you're concerned that training will disrupt your productivity and product support will be poor?"

4. "Really? Could you tell me more?"

Answer:

Option 1: This option is incorrect. Adam should restate the prospect's objections in his own words to clarify the issues before empathizing with Charles.

Option 2: This is an incorrect option. Because Adam has already heard details about the customer support issues, he shouldn't ask specific questions to delve further into the problem at this point.

Option 3: This is the correct option. After listening and clarifying the issues, Adam should restate the prospect's objections in his own words to confirm his understanding.

Option 4: This is an incorrect option. Adam has already listened to the details of the issues and shouldn't invite more details at this point.

Case Study: Question 2 of 2

Adam has now restated the prospect's objections.

What would be the most appropriate thing for him to say next?

Options:

1. "So to be clear, your main concern is about support quality? And lost productivity?"

2. "We can certainly expedite the training and guarantee you optimal quality support. Is anything else worrying you?"

3. "I'd also be upset with such poor helpdesk support, but I assure you, we dealt with those issues long ago."

4. "Our training usually takes two full days, which really isn't a long time. Or is that too long for you?"

Answer:

Option 1: This is an incorrect option. Adam has already restated the prospect's objections. He shouldn't do so a second time.

Option 2: This option is correct. Adam should isolate the objections that have been voiced and find out if the prospect has any further objections.

Option 3: This is a correct option. Adam should empathize with Charles to show concern.

Option 4: This option is incorrect. With the prospect's objection clarified, Adam shouldn't be asking more questions about it at this point.

KEY STRATEGIES FOR CLOSING A SALE

Key strategies for closing a sale

Closing techniques

To help move a sales discussion toward a sale, you can use a "trial close", which tests the attitude or opinion of your prospect. You ask the prospect a high-level question to gauge how close you are to the sale. For example, you might ask, "Do you think you'd benefit from this?" or "Does this sound like something you're interested in?" You then allow the prospect to respond, remaining silent and waiting for an answer, even if it takes a while to come.

The prospect's answer will indicate what you need to do next. If the prospect raises queries, it means there are still unresolved objections to deal with.

In such cases, you should ask the prospect about the issues and follow the sales objections process to deal with the objections.

If the prospect raises no objections, you can use one of various techniques to close the sale.

You may have used various closing techniques in the past. Three popular types are the summary technique, the assumption technique, and the choice technique.

The summary technique

To use the summary technique, you summarize your offering for the prospect. You list each aspect of the offering separately, making the collective deal sound like a bigger package than the sum of its parts.

Once you've completed your summary, you ask the prospect if there's anything else that you need to cover. If the answer is no, you can close the deal.

When using the summary technique, you should emphasize how the prospect will benefit from your offering – for example, through improved efficiency or reduced costs.

It's important to keep the prospect interested, so don't go into excessive detail. Instead make your points clearly and concisely.

The summary technique is most effective when a prospect has already acknowledged the value of your offering. It's also useful when the conversation has drifted off track and you need to steer it back to the sale.

It's now time for Bhadrak to try closing the sale of the information management system to Joe. There are different techniques he could use. First consider the summary technique.

Follow along to find out how Bhadrak progresses.

Bhadrak: As we discussed, the portal covers end-to-end communication. *Bhadrak is explaining.*

Joe: Yes...that's what you mentioned. *Joe is hesitant.*

Essential Selling Skills

Bhadrak: It's also got automated workflow for documents, and mobile phone alerts to let people know when their input is needed. That should cut out unnecessary delays. *Bhadrak is showing Joe his notes.*

Bhadrak: And it gives you huge online storage - all your drawings and plans for contractors and inspectors to access from anywhere. *Bhadrak is enthusiastic.*

Bhadrak: The audit trails mean you can avoid disputes with contractors. It addresses all your needs! *Bhadrak is enthusiastic.*

Joe: Yes, I can see that now. *Joe is confident and focused.*

Bhadrak: Have I left anything out? Any other concerns? *Bhadrak is confident.*

Joe: No...no, I think you've covered everything. *Joe is impressed.*

Bhadrak: Great! Let's finalize the last few details, and we're set. *Bhadrak is enthusiastic.*

Question
What summary technique guidelines did Bhadrak apply in wrapping up the deal?

Options:
1. He explained the technical details of the solution
2. He confirmed that no other objections remained
3. He listed the features of the system
4. He kept the closing concise and exciting
5. He listened closely to Joe's objections

Answer:
Option 1: This is an incorrect option. Bhadrak didn't get technical at this stage. Instead, he tied the product's features to benefits Joe's company could reap.

Option 2: This option is correct. After listing all the features, Bhadrak asked Joe if there was anything else to be discussed.

Option 3: This option is correct. Bhadrak systematically mentioned each of the features that were included in the product.

Option 4: This is a correct option. Bhadrak's closing briefly explained the benefit of each feature. He was clearly enthusiastic, finishing off with an optimistic statement.

Option 5: This option is incorrect. At the point of closing the sale, every one of Joe's objections had been resolved.

The assumption technique

In the assumption technique, you don't wait for the prospect to show willingness to buy and you don't directly ask for a sale either.

You simply assume that the prospect has agreed to buy and then pursue a line of questioning related to the details of the sale. For example, you might ask about the quantity to be purchased, delivery dates, and payment terms.

The assumption technique relies heavily on momentum and continuity – meaning that after you've received an answer, you should immediately move on to the next question. In this way, you direct the prospect to a sale, keeping things moving and reducing the chances of the sale stalling or breaking down.

The assumption technique is most effective after you've completed the preceding steps of the sales process and you're confident that the prospect recognizes the value in your product or service.

Of course, prospects might still raise objections or ask questions during this type of close. If this occurs, handle the objections appropriately and then immediately resume your line of questioning.

Bhadrak could also have used the assumption technique in closing his sale with Joe. Consider how this might have worked.

Follow along as Bhadrak tries using the assumption technique to close the sale.

Bhadrak: So I'll need your input about the implementation. *Bhadrak is confident.*

Joe: Oh OK....What do you need to know? *Joe is confused.*

Bhadrak: How quickly do you need the system in place? When would be a good time to install? *Bhadrak is confident.*

Joe: Well...we're swamped at the moment, so I'd say wait another...two weeks? *Joe is hesitant.*

Bhadrak: Great. And what about payment terms? *Bhadrak is enthusiastic, and makes a note in his notebook.*

Joe: Finance has a strict policy – thirty days net after installation is signed off. *Joe is more assured.*

Bhadrak: That will work. Give me a few minutes, I'll have the contract printed. *Bhadrak is enthusiastic and Joe is agreeable.*

Question

How did Bhadrak apply the assumption technique in this case?

Options:

1. He waited for Joe to ask about installation details
2. He immediately started asking Joe questions about the implementation

3. He waited for Joe to ask about payment details

4. He asked Joe if he'd like to purchase the system

Answer:

Option 1: This option is incorrect. Bhadrak didn't wait for Joe to raise questions about installation. He assumed Joe was interested – which is a sign of the assumption technique – and asked the questions himself.

Option 2: This is the correct option. Bhadrak assumed that Joe would be buying and immediately started asking questions related to the sale.

Option 3: This is an incorrect option. Bhadrak didn't wait for Joe to raise questions about payment. He assumed Joe was interested – which is a sign of the assumption technique – and asked the questions himself.

Option 4: This is an incorrect option. Bhadrak didn't ask Joe if he was interested. He simply assumed that Joe would make a purchase.

The choice technique

The choice technique involves giving a prospect different options to choose from. Choices could be related to aspects such as product model, size, color, service plan, delivery, price, and payment terms.

The choice technique encourages prospects to be involved and takes some pressure off them by offering alternatives, rather than presenting just one option and asking for a commitment to it.

When using this technique, it's important to present only choices that you're comfortable with. Don't offer the prospect an option that would be difficult for you – for example, same-day delivery when you know that you'll need to source stock from another city.

Now consider how the choice technique might have worked for Bhadrak when closing his sale.

Follow along as Bhadrak uses the choice technique to close the sale.

Bhadrak: Why don't we start implementation around the middle of the month? Or is month end better? *Bhadrak is confident and slightly pushy.*

Joe: Um...month ends are hectic. The middle is more manageable. Will this disrupt things much? *Joe is more assured, but is still anxious.*

Bhadrak: We'll avoid that by working when fewer people are in the office. What about early morning, or late afternoon? Which would you prefer? *Bhadrak is reassuring.*

Joe: Most of our folks are in pretty early, but they leave by four, so late afternoon is perfect. *Joe is relieved.*

Bhadrak: Great. So I'll just finalize the paperwork and send it on. *Bhadrak and Joe are both pleased.*

In this case, Bhadrak gave Joe a choice between installation dates and he also gave Joe specific choices regarding installation times. By showing sensitivity to Joe's scheduling needs and putting his mind at ease about major interruptions to the office environment, Bhadrak was able to close the deal.

Question

Match closing techniques with the corresponding examples. Not all the examples of dialog will have a match.

Options:
A. Summary technique
B. Assumption technique
C. Choice technique

Targets:

1. "We'll present five interactive workshops on your premises, include high-quality worksheets and handouts, and run individual sessions with employees that require them."

2. "I think the reception area is the optimal place to put it. Would 10 a.m. suit you for our delivery?"

3. "So, which style works better for you? The Classic or the New Age? Blue or Black?"

4. "You'll probably need time to consider everything. Shall I give you a call next week?"

Answer:

By listing the parts of the offering one after the other, the summary technique makes the deal sound bigger than the sum of the individual parts.

The assumption technique assumes the prospect has already decided to buy, and then continues the conversation, leading the prospect to the final details of the sale.

The choice technique gets the prospect involved by offering options related to some aspect of the product and asking for a decision.

The summary, assumption, and choice techniques don't give the prospect time to decide.

Sales objections are a normal part of the sales process, so it's important to view them optimistically and be prepared for them. A good general process for dealing with objections is to listen, question, restate, empathize, and then resolve the objections.

To advance a sales discussion, you can use a trial close, followed by the closing technique that's most appropriate for the situation. Popular closing techniques include the summary, assumption, and choice techniques.

HOW TO FOLLOW UP AFTER A SALE

How to follow up after a sale

Following up with customers

After closing sales, salespeople often fail to follow up with their customers. Some simply forget, while others fear that they'll seem pushy. Some salespeople just don't recognize the return that following up can yield.

Developing lasting relationships is critical to long-term success in sales. Good relationships can lead to repeat sales, as well as word-of-mouth advertising. So after you've closed a sale, it's important to maintain your relationship by following up.

Following up with a customer can have several benefits. These include differentiating you from your competitors, generating repeat business, improving the customer's confidence in the purchasing decision, and aiding your market research.

See each benefit for more information about it.

Differentiates you

Following up can differentiate you from your competitors. It shows that you care about the customer and whether your product or service is meeting this person's needs. This contrasts with salespeople who seem to forget about the customer once they've closed the deal.

Generates repeat business

Following up helps you stay in touch with customers' needs and keeps your name in their minds, making it more likely that they will purchase from you again.

Improves customer confidence

After a sale is concluded, a customer may start having "buyer's remorse" – doubts or regrets about the decision to buy. You can mitigate this by following up. Your extra efforts after the sale help show that you believe in the product or service you've sold.

Aids market research

Following up with customers can teach you about how their business needs are changing. You can then enhance or add to your offerings to meet those needs, for both existing and new customers.

Continuous direct contact with customers also helps you learn how they make purchasing decisions and how to make your marketing efforts more effective.

To reap the benefits of a follow-up, you should follow several guidelines. Some of these guidelines are to make yourself available, express gratitude, reinforce the benefits of the transaction, and get feedback and make recommendations.

Making yourself available includes regularly contacting your customers to let them know you can assist them further. This assistance could relate to the product or service you've sold.

And it's important to show genuine willingness to help and to avoid trying to sell the customers something else.

Doing this builds a positive impression in the mind of a customer, because you portray yourself as a helpful individual who's making an extra effort to assist customers with their needs – even if there's no obvious financial gain involved.

When customers need to make purchases in other areas, you can use your professional network to recommend sellers to them.

For example, if a customer wants to remodel an office environment, you might help by saying, "I've got a client in the interior design industry that would be happy to assist. Mention my name and you may even get a discount!"

This enhances your relationship, helping ensure you become a resource the customer can call on for advice in the future.

Follow-up media

Your answer may have included phone calls, e-mails, visits, and even handwritten notes or cards. You can use all of these to follow up on sales.

However, although a quick e-mail or telephone call will do the job, you can enhance the positive effects of following up on a sale by sending a handwritten note or card. This is more personal and makes it clear you appreciate your customer's business.

Everyone likes to be thanked. So a simple thank-you note or message is important. For example, you could write "Thanks so much for your recent purchase. It was a pleasure doing business with you and I look forward to working with you in future."

Attach your business card to your message so the customer has a record of your contact details, and a reminder of your products or services.

It's important to reinforce the benefits of the sale because buyer's remorse can plague customers after they've purchased. Be sure to promote the merits of the product or service you've sold. For example, say a customer purchased a fleet of your delivery vans. You could send the customer statistics showing how sales of the same vans are rising each month, to make it clear that the buyer's decision was in line with industry trends.

Another avenue of following up is getting feedback from customers and making recommendations to them. You can send customers surveys or feedback forms to gather valuable information about their reactions to your product or service.

Or you could use follow-ups to recommend complementary products or services that customers may be interested in. For example, if you've sold barcode scanners to a retailer, you could follow up by recommending digital price tags as the next purchase.

As part of the process of seeking feedback, you can also ask customers for referrals.

Question

Karla's organization has just installed its proprietary enterprise resource planning system at a major oil company.

Which techniques are effective ways for Karla to follow up the sale?

Options:

1. Invite the client to a ceremony where the company receives a reward for the system

2. Ask the client to report the system's performance every three months

3. Send the client a handwritten thank-you message

4. Record the client's details in a "Future sales" file

5. Recommend that the client add a customizable reporting component to the system

6. Ask the client to contact her directly if any queries arise

Answer:

Option 1: This is a correct option. Karla can reinforce the benefits of the purchase, helping overcome any doubts the customer has, by letting the customer know about the award.

Option 2: This option is incorrect. Karla, rather than the client, should take responsibility for following up regularly.

Option 3: This option is correct. Karla can express gratitude via a card or letter, with her business card attached.

Option 4: This is an incorrect option. To be beneficial, following up on a sale has to involve making contact with the customer. This is separate from purely administrative tasks like recording client details.

Option 5: This is a correct option. Karla can use a follow-up as an opportunity to recommend other products or services that the client may be interested in.

Option 6: This option is correct. Karla should make it clear that she's available to help the client, and show a genuine willingness to help.

Following up on sales can help differentiate you from competitors, generate repeat business, improve customers' confidence, and aid in your market research.

When following up, you should make it clear that you're available to help the customer, express gratitude, reinforce the benefits of the customer's purchase, and use the opportunity to ask for feedback and provide recommendations.

REFERENCES

References

Smart Calling: Eliminate the Fear, Failure, and Rejection From Cold Calling - 2010, Art Sobczak, John Wiley & Sons
Value-added Selling: How to Sell More Profitably, Confidently, and Professionally by Competing on Value, Not Price, Third Edition - 2010, Tom Reilly, McGraw-Hill
Smart Selling on the Phone and Online: Inside Sales That Gets Results - 2009, Josiane Chriqui Feigon
Cold Calling Techniques: (That Really Work!), Fifth Edition - 2003, Stephan Schiffman, Adams Media
Heat up Your Cold Calls: How to Make Prospects Listen, Respond, and Buy - 2005, George R. Walther, Kaplan Professional
Red-Hot Cold Call Selling: Prospecting Techniques That Really Pay Off, Second Edition - 2006, Paul S. Goldner

Lessons from 100,000 Cold Calls: Selling Techniques That Work... No Matter How Many Calls You Make - 2008, Stewart Rogers, Sourcebooks

Knock Your Socks Off Prospecting: How to Cold Call, Get Qualified Leads, and Make More Money - 2005, William "Skip" Miller and Ron Zemke

How to Sell without Being a JERK!: The Foolproof Approach to the World's Second Oldest Profession - 2008, John Klymshyn, John Wiley & Sons

The Fisherman's Guide to Selling: Reel in the Sale: Hook, Line, and Sinker - 2007, Joseph DiMisa, Adams Media

Selling by Objectives - 1998, Anthony Alessandra, Jim Cathcart and Phillip Wexler, Tony Alessandra

10 Steps to Sales Success: The Proven System That Can Shorten the Selling Cycle, Double Your Close Ratio, and Significantly Increase Your Income - 2003, Tim Breithaupt

Perfect Selling: Open The Door. Close The Deal - 2008, Linda Richardson, McGraw-Hill

Red-Hot Selling: Power Techniques That Win Even the Toughest Sale - 2010, Paul S. Goldner

Rain Making: Attract New Clients No Matter What Your Field, 2nd Edition - 2008, Ford Harding, Adams Media

Selling Professional Services to the Fortune 500: How to Win in the Billion-Dollar Market of Strategy Consulting, Technology Solutions, and Outsourcing Services - 2010, Gary S. Luefschuetz, McGraw-Hill

10 Steps to Successful Sales - 2010, Brian Lambert, ASTD

Kick Your Own Ass: The Will, Skill, and Drill of Selling More Than You Ever Thought Possible - 2010, Robert Early Johnson, John Wiley & Sons

Magnetic Selling: Develop the Charm and Charisma that Attract Customers and Maximize Sales - 2006, Robert W. Bly

Perfect Phrases for Sales Presentations: Hundreds of Ready-to-Use Phrases for Delivering Powerful Presentations That Close Every Sale - 2010, Linda Eve Diamond, McGraw-Hill

How You Make the Sale: What Every New Salesperson Needs to Know - 2005, Frank McNair, Sourcebooks

Collaborative Selling: How to Gain the Competitive Advantage in Sales - 1993, Tony Alessandra and Rick Barrera, Tony Alessandra

Value-added Selling: How to Sell More Profitably, Confidently, and Professionally by Competing on Value, Not Price, Third Edition - 2010, Tom Reilly, McGraw-Hill

Get Clients Now!: A 28-Day Marketing Program for Professionals, Consultants, and Coaches, Second Edition - 2007, C. J. Hayden

Soft Sell: The New Art of Selling - 2003, Tim Connor, Sourcebooks

GLOSSARY

Glossary

C

cold call - An unsolicited phone call made with no previous priming of a prospect to find out if the person would be interested in developing a business relationship, or in a product or service.

G

gatekeeper - Someone, such as a personal assistant, receptionist, or administrator, who screens calls for a prospect.

I

inquiry - A request for information or help about a product or service. The person making the inquiry won't necessarily be interested in what you have to offer.

N

need - A gap between an actual and a desired state.

O

objection - An argument against a given proposition.

P

prospect - A potential client or customer.

Q

qualification meeting - A meeting between salesperson and prospect, during which the salesperson attempts to qualify the prospect. This involves determining whether the prospect is able and likely to make a purchase.

qualified sales lead - A prospect who's interested in a product or service you're selling, and who's both likely and able to make a purchase. The prospect may also be a source of profitable business opportunities and referrals in the future.

S

sales lead - A potential customer, or prospect, who is interested in what you're selling.

script - An outline or sketch of what you want to say to a prospect during a cold call. It should contain all the important details and points you want to cover.

solution - A product or service that meets a customer's need.

solution objective - A change that should occur as a result of a solution. Solution objectives should be specific, measurable, attainable, and complementary.

T

trial close - The use of a high-level question to test how ready a prospect is to buy.

V

value proposition - The benefits, or value, you offer a prospect in return for buying a product or service. This should be based on your company's operating philosophy and actual results, and should give customers real facts and figures to demonstrate the tangible results they can gain.

www.ingramcontent.com/pod-product-compliance
Lightning Source LLC
Chambersburg PA
CBHW020924180526
45163CB00007B/2867